VERDUN: VISION AND COMPREHENSION
THE BATTLEFIELD AND ITS SURROUNDINGS

Entirely conceived by, and photographs by, EDITIONS
MAGE

Rights of total or partial reproduction and translation reserved.

Copyright of this edition for photographs and text: © EDITORIAL ESCUDO DE ORO, S.A. - Palaudarias, 26 - Barcelona (Spain).

4th Edition, February 1985

I.S.B.N.

English 84-378-1005-1

Dep. Legal B. 5064-1985

DISTRIBUTOR: EDITIONS MAGE
36 rue Henri Fournier, 93700 DRANCY (FRANCE)
Telephone: 831 52 47

Impreso en España - Printed in Spain
F.I.S.A. Palaudarias, 26 - Barcelona-4

An aerial view of the original site, showing the Cathedral with the ground plan forming the shape of a cross of Lorraine, the Cloister and the Bishop's Palace. One can see the city's concentrical formation, the covered market and — spanning a branch of the Meuse in the background — the Pont Couvert.

VERDUN: FROM THE TOWN'S ORIGINS TO MODERN TIMES

The site

The original site of VERDUN is a steep promontory running from east to west and abutting on the bank of the river Meuse. This outpost dominating the river was inhabited at a very early date, apparently around the 3rd century B.C., and became an important Gallic fortress (Verdun means "powerful fortress"). This stronghold, so easy to defend, was the heart of the town in ancient times and is now occupied by all the higher part of the old town and, particularly, by the Cathedral. The town's strategical importance augmented in Roman times, for it effectively controls all movement on the road between Rheims and Metz. The town prospered under Roman rule and very soon expanded towards the south-east, occupying the width of the valley; a tradesmen's quarter, the *macellum* or food market, grew up between the river and the foot of the hill below the *castrum,* where Rue Mazel is today. Access from this area to the high part of the town, on top of the rocky promontory, has always been by means of two steep, narrow streets now known as *Les Gros Degrés* and Rue Châtel.

The town's lay-out in the Middle Ages

Verdun was a Roman town from the 3rd century onwards, becoming the see of a bishopric dependant on

Tour St. Vanne (12th century), the only surviving vestige of the famous St. Vanne Abbey, established on the site of the present-day Citadel.

Trèves (as were also Metz and Toul) in the 4th century; the town later passed into the control of the Franks and, subsequently, the Carolingians. The treaty of Verdun dismantled Charlemagne's Empire in 843 and the town was granted to Lothaire; it was finally annexed to the *Basse Lorraine* duchy in the 10th century and formed part of the Germanic Empire until 1552. About this time — in 952 — Bishop Berenger founded the Abbey of Saint Vanne on a hill to the west of the town (now the Citadel) and dedicated it to Saint Benoît. Around 1200 Abbot Louis de Hirgis enriched this abbey with a vast church, of which only one tower remains: a fine specimen of Romanesque architecture later integrated into a splendid late Gothic church which was unfortunately demolished around 1830.

Throughout the height of the Middle Ages the *castrum* in the high part of the town was only surrounded by primitive ramparts; all trace of these has disappeared but aerial photography has admirably defined the original site and the demarcation of its edifices, distributed as dictated by geography.

In the 10th century, Verdun — with its Saint Vanne Abbey which the felicitous King Richard (1004-1046) transformed into one of the most famous communities in the West — was annexed to the Germanic Empire and played its part in a new civilization which sprang from the heritage of the Carolingian world. The town became an important centre for culture towards the year 1000. In 1048, as a result of a feudal war between the Duke of the *Haute Lorraine,* Godefroy le Barbu ("the bearded"), and the Emperor

The Cathedral's Romanesque east transept.

The Cathedral: "Lion Doorway."

A side chapel in the Crypt, with polychrome capitals. ▷

Henri III, the Cathedral was set alight and the reconstruction of the monument as we now know it was decided upon. The building is on the whole Romanesque, principally 11th and 12th centuries, as is demonstrated by the windows in the east transept — the capitals are carved with acanthus leaves — and by the great crypt. This latter was filled in as a result of a fire in 1755, but after the first World War it was restored and now appears as one of the most perfect creations of Romanesque art, explaining the influence exerted by the architect, Garin, even on the building of Trèves Cathedral. The *Portail du Lion* ("Lion's Doorway") was bricked up in the 18th century, it

displays the influence of Burgundian art. The statue of Christ appears surrounded by the four animals symbolising the evangelists and despite its greater heaviness, bears a resemblance to the doorway at Paray le Monial or to a rather weak version of the themes sculptured on the narthex at Vézelay.

The east crypt (the great crypt) is divided into a nave and two nave aisles of five bays each; pillars made up of four columns separate the nave from the aisles. When, after the first World War, it was restored to the design it had before its collapse due to the fire of 1755, the architects used the old Romanesque capitals which still survive, attached to the walls.

SALUS INFIRMORUM O.P.N.

The Cathedral's East Crypt — also called the Great Crypt
— which was filled in as a result of the fire of 1755 and
reopened after the first World War.

Three of the thirteen modern capitals given over to the
Battle of Verdun, adorning the Crypt. They were
sculptured by Le Bourgeois (1935) and simply, movingly,
depict life in the trenches with its sufferings, the presence
of death, its dramas, including the execution of a soldier
— this scene has never been represented elsewhere.

The Cathedral Cloister, a marvel of French art.

These capitals recall Burgundian art, as do those of the east choir and also the polychrome capitals in one of the crypt's lateral chapels. Le Bourgeois, the sculptor, embellished the crypt with a series of modern capitals in 1935, in conformity with the Romanesque capitals' shape and size; some of the new ones are devoted to the Church of Verdun and others — thirteen of them — to the Battle of Verdun. The simple, moving motifs depicted in stone evoke various scenes of life in the trenches, the sufferings and death of the soldiers and problems concerning artillery, forts and the evacuation of the wounded. In its pitiless precision the sober imagery even shows the execution of a soldier, a scene that has never been depicted elsewhere.

The Porte Châtel (12th century), the oldest gate and the only surviving vestige of the Fermeté or mediaeval ring of fortifications. This is the highest point in the upper part of the city.

The Porte Chaussée (1380), the key edifice of the grand rempart, *a remarkable specimen of mediaeval military architecture.*

The cloister

The cloister is a marvel of French art lying on the south side of the Cathedral. It comprises three arcades with a total length of 82 metres, the main arcade accounts for 40 m. Despite the harmony of the ensemble, suggesting that it was all built at one time, the building owes a lot to the 16th century for the general characteristics of the late Gothic style deployed in the archways. But the arches in the east part — the first reached by the visitor — go back to the 14th century. The roof-bosses display abundant,

original adornments whose composite motifs range from floral and mythological themes to the satirical style. The cloister, previously a burial ground for canons (some memorial inscriptions may still be seen), was surrounded by the chapter halls, school, library and chapter prison.

The city walls in the Middle Ages

Just like any other mediaeval city, the people of Verdun thought at a very early stage to protect the city with fortified ramparts. The original fortress, or Roman *castrum* (2nd century), was replaced in mediaeval times by a ring of ramparts called *Fermeté*, only the 12th century *Porte Châtel* gate has survived from this structure. In the 13th century the necessity of protecting the lower-lying traders' area, Mazel (*macellum* = market), imposed the construction of the *petit rempart* (''little rampart''), this was replaced in later centuries by the *grand rempart;* the *Porte Chaussée* (1380), which was built at the expense of Wautrec, the dean of Verdun's markets, is the most important part of this fortification. This gate is really a small castle made up of two large round towers of three storeys each, carefully connected to and joined by a central section. The platform between the towers has a crenellated parapet with machicolation. The heavy wooden portcullis, reinforced with metal, may still be seen under the entrance arch, for this was a military prison from 1754 to 1890. The *Porte Chaussée* is classified as an historical monument, and remains a remarkable example of mediaeval military architecture.

The *grand rempart,* which was built in the 14th and 15th centuries and within encloses not only the traders' area in the lower part of the city, but also Saint Vanne and Saint Airy abbeys, themselves already fortified. This ensemble was all the more imposing by virtue of the fact that the curtains of the ramparts — of which an impressive part remains — were interspersed by numerous towers; the *Tour des Plaides* and the *Tour de l'Islot* are fine examples. If the

Tour de l'Islot.

Tour des Plaids.

The Tour de l'Islot *and the* Tour des Plaids *are two examples of the towers which flanked the curtains of the* grand rempart *(14th and 15th centuries).*

second is only a flanking tower, tradition situates Verdun's local custom-law court in the first, whence its name ("Litigation Tower"). Sheltered behind these walls the city was able to avoid the brunt of the Hundred Years' War and of the feudal wars occasioned by the great Western schism; and to enjoy an economic recovery in the 15th and 16th centuries, as is witnessed by the splendid private house of the Dean of the Chapter *(le Primicier),* second in rank to the Bishop. After the first World War, this elegant Renaissance building, in the Italian style with an interior gallery over a cloister, became Verdun's municipal museum, called *de la Princerie* (a deformation of *Primicier*).

Apart from the building's architecture — the arrangement of the interior is not without interest — the museum displays a beautiful liturgical comb finely worked in ivory, attributed to the Emperor Henri II, and an interesting collection of mediaeval statues, part of which is from Mont devant Sassey (for example, a striking Bound Christ), whereas the contemporary era and the traditions of Lorraine are represented by Argonne china and by the room devoted to sugared almonds. This highly-reputed local confectionery was known in the Middle Ages and was originally produced for medical use by the apothecaries' guild.

The Princerie *Museum — a* Renaissance building with its interior gallery above a cloister — houses the municipal museum of Lorraine Arts and Traditions.

Princerie *Museum:*
Lorraine furniture,
Argonne china.

A wooden statue of Saint Nicolas, the patron Saint of Lorraine.

A seated Virgin Mary in polychrome stone (12th century).

Above: the tomb of Saintignon and his wife (16th century).

Below: the room devoted to sugared almonds, a highly reputed local item of confectionery that has been produced since the Middle Ages.

A finely-worked liturgical comb of ivory attributed to Emperor Henri II (11½ × 8½ cm).

An old door at 15 Rue des Prêtres (probably altered at the time of the Renaissance) with its pilasters and support decorated with geometrical designs surmounted by cooking pots and a niche (16th century).

The towers of Notre-Dame Cathedral and the doorway of the Grand Séminaire.

CLASSICAL VERDUN

The Cathedral

Although the Romanesque Cathedral's original ground-plan (Rhenish-type basilica with the nave and lower parts enclosed between two transepts and, behind these, a polygonal choir to the east and a level chevet to the west) has survived intact, the building's interior has been considerably modified over the centuries. In the 13th and 14th centuries the panelled ceilings were replaced by Gothic vaults and nine chapels were installed between the buttresses of the aisles. Until the 18th century, however, the magnificent building, more than 100 metres long, retained its four spires. The fire in 1755 was the pretext for alterations which not only eliminated the spires, replacing them with the rectangular towers at the west end, and involved filling in the crypt, but also disfigured the whole of the cathedral's interior with neoclassical decoration and replaced the Gothic doorways with cold, impersonal entrances. This adaptation to contemporary taste was not compensated for by the admirable choir-stalls and woodwork installed at this juncture any more than it was by the cumbersome baldachin (a copy of the Bernin baldachin in Rome) which interrupts the nave's perspective. The Cathedral was damaged by the shelling attacks of 1916, which revealed parts obscured by masonry in the 18th century, and was subsequently subjected to a remarkable restoration process which uncovered the original Romanesque architecture. One may see, among other things, the very beautiful doorway called *de l'Officialité* at the foot of the north-west tower, which is pure 11th century Romanesque and recalls to a certain extent the severe Cistercian style of architecture.

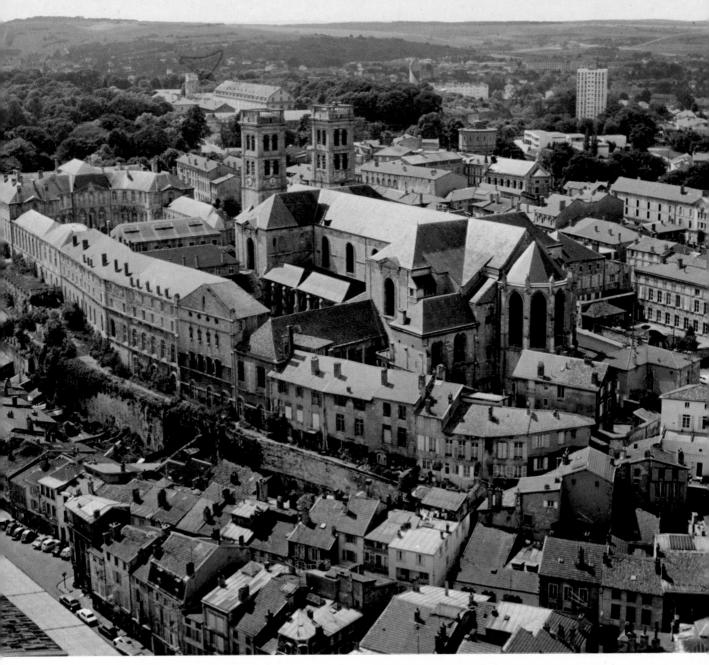

*An over-all view of Notre-Dame Cathedral, the cloister
and the Bishop's Palace, towering over the lower part of
the city from the top of the ramparts.*

The
Cathedral
nave.

The courtyard side of the Bishop's Palace (18th century).

The Bishop's Palace

The present-day Palace was built during the episcopates of Monseigneur d'Hallencourt (1723-1754) and Mgr Nicolaï (1754-1769). Mgr Desnos, the last Bishop of Verdun under the *Ancien Régime* (pre-1789; he died at Koblenz after having emigrated) concluded the work. This stern, elegant edifice was raised largely on the site of the old Renaissance Palace built by Nicolas Psaume (Bishop from 1548 to 1575), a more modest building that was about to fall in ruins at the start of the 18th century. Mgr d'Hallencourt — whose monogram may still be seen on the pediments of the doorways — originally intended to restore the old edifice, using the revenue

provided by the transfer of part of the Bishopric's woodland. The King's architect, Robert de Cotte, was summoned and he considered that it was preferable to raze the whole and build a new palace. The building works began in 1725 under the supervision of the self-same Robert de Cotte; after his death in 1739 his son supervised them. Louis XV was able to stay there on passing through Verdun in 1744. Under the Empire the building was assigned to the estate of the senator for Nancy. The generals commanding the Meuse *département* had their headquarters there from 1814 onwards but when the episcopal see was re-established in 1823 the Bishop's Palace once again became the Bishop's residence. Mgr Ginisty — the founder of Douaumont — reoccupied the building

The Bishop's Palace gardens.

Above: the Bishop's private chapel. ▷

The Hôtel de Ville *(Town Hall, 17th century):*
Below right: the Court of Honour with the four cannons
awarded by the government after the siege of 1870.
Below left: the room with the books that record the
names of those who fought at Verdun.

after its restoration in 1935. The Palace has been classified as an historical monument since 1923 and still houses the episcopal see of Verdun and the municipal library.

When Robert de Cotte drew up the plans for the Bishop's Palace, he deployed great skill in accomodating, in a relatively restricted space, a main building with high roof flanked by two projecting wings. The main storey is preceded by a raised ground floor and a first floor with discreet, elegant decoration. With the repetition of semicircular figures at the entrance and in front of the exterior flight of steps, the courtyard side gives an impression of more space than there really is; and the stern, perfect façade gives on to the typical French gardens. In the south wing, the Bishop's private Chapel retains its original décor, with two paintings by the 18th century Lorraine artist Mansuy: *Agonie* ("Christ Dying") and the "Resurrection". Other canvases by the same painter, with mythological themes, may be seen in the Bishop's old library above the elegant wainscotting at the western end of the great gallery.

The side giving on to the Hôtel de Ville *gardens.*

Hôtel de Ville

The City Hall precedes the Bishop's Palace by a good century of classical art; it is an elegant Louis XIII building greatly influenced by the Italian style. The *Hôtel de Ville* was built by a rich gunpowder trader, Nicolas Japin, in 1625, by the old Roman road in the lower part of town. The legend has it that this dwelling was intended for Marie de Médicis who, having fallen out with Richelieu, planned to take refuge in it… The municipal authorities of Verdun were installed there in 1738. The main body of the building connects two wings, also joined by a terrace giving on to the road, its decoration is a felicitous combination of sculptures and protruding stones with bluntened edges. The façade gives on to the gardens, which are reached via a terrace and a very fine staircase with balustrades. It was in this elegant palace — home of the community's history and tradition — that Lieutenant-Colonel Beaurepaire committed suicide on the night of the 1st September 1792, rather than countenance the surrender of the city under his command. A happier memory is the siege which the people of Verdun actively resisted from the 24th August to the 9th November 1870. In 1873, in homage to this fine defence, the government awarded the city the four cannons now on display in the court of honour. The books containing the list of servicemen who fought at Verdun and the medals and mementos presented to the city by sympathetic countries after the first World War are kept on show in the rooms of the *Hôtel de Ville.*

Hôtel de Ville: *the room housing the flags and decorations.*

The Porte du Secours, *also called the Field-Marshals' Gate, a reference to the sixteen monumental stone statues depicting French generals and field-marshals which are to be found in the gardens backing on to the Vauban rampart.*

Chapelle du Collège.

The Chapelle du Collège

The *Chapelle du Collège,* also called the Jesuits'
chapel (for it dates from the time when they ran the
college) is contemporary with the Bishop's Palace, it
was built from 1731 to 1735. The elegant, balanced
façade, built in the neoclassical style, was favourably
set off when the reconstruction of Verdun after 1920
made it possible to clear and widen the Rue Saint
Pierre. The interior of the Chapel comprises a nave
and two nave aisles, the vaults supported by tapering
columns with Ionic capitals. The modern windows are
by the master artist in stained glass, Grüber from
Nancy, to whom we also owe many of the stained

Above and below: casemates in the Citadel.

Centre: a bartizan in the rampart of the Citadel.

Aerial view of the Citadel.

glass windows in the Cathedral. The heart of Bishop Nicolas Psaume, the founder of the college (1570) and architect of Verdun's reintegration to France in 1552, reposes in the choir, which was restored after being damaged by shelling on the 1st September 1944.

Verdun and War

These religious foundations should not make us forget that Verdun was to remain a place of war for a long time to come. The first citadel was built in the 16th century. France's occupation of Verdun was bound to cause a reaction on the part of the Holy Roman Emperor Charles the Fifth: he laid siege to Metz in October 1552. *Maréchal* (Marshal) de Tavarnes sketched the first outlines of a citadel when he was governor of Verdun, its construction was undertaken from 1567 to 1591 and later, under the direction of *Maréchal* de Marillac, from 1624 onwards. In 1648, however, the treaty of Munster assigned Verdun definitively to France; and Vauban reviewed the whole fortification from 1664 onwards, so as to guarantee communications for the armies and for Flanders: he conceived an ambitious plan which supplemented the Citadel with a bastioned wall right around the city. The glacis and counterscarps survive to this day, and the Gates (Saint Victor, *de France*

Above: Saint Victor Gate.

Below: Porte du Champ, *an ancient twin tower forming part of the* grand rempart.

The Porte de France: *the gate-keeper's lodge survives.*

An aerial view of S Paul's Gate, the Rue St. Paul and the former S Paul's Abbey, now occupied by the Law Courts and the police headquarters.

and *du Secours,* also called *des Maréchaux*) are still as many entrances to the heart of the city. The *Porte du Champ,* interestingly enough, is an old twin tower similar to the *Tour Chaussée:* it forms part of the *grand rempart* and was lowered and refitted by Vauban and subsequently modified at the end of the 19th century. The *Porte Saint Paul* is modern: it was opened up in the bastioned rampart in 1877, so as to enable the people of Verdun to go to the recently constructed railway station. A bronze monument cast following a model by Rodin stands in front of the gate, which also affords access to the present-day *Palais de Justice* (law-courts), an elegant edifice of brick and ashlars which was previously the *Abbaye Saint Paul* (S Paul's Abbey), of the *Prémontrés* Order, rebuilt in the 18th century. The Sub-Prefecture next-door occupies an older, predominantly Renaissance building.

S Paul's Gate (1877) and the bronze monument cast after a model by Rodin, a gift of Holland. An inscription narrates the trials suffered by the city from 450 to 1916.

The Victory Monument backs on to the old 12th-century rampart. It was inaugurated on the 23rd June 1929.

VERDUN TODAY

The great turmoil of 1916 effected deep changes in the city's lay-out, and the memory of this unique confrontation extended its renown. Verdun was partially evacuated in 1914, then completely in February 1916; being a communications centre and logistical base, it suffered considerably from shelling by long-range artillery. An intense period of reconstruction altered the city's appearance on the return of the inhabitants after the conflict. The Rue Mazel was widened, accomodating the Victory Monument in the middle: its steps and the upper crypt housing the Golden Book of those decorated at Verdun (including the Americans at Saint-Mihiel and Argonne, and of 1944) are built on to the old 12th century rampart. The

Monument was inaugurated on the 23rd June 1929. The crypt is framed by two Russian cannons cast in Perm which were captured from the Russian army by the Germans and recaptured by the French. A torch is lit at the Arc de Triomphe and deposited in the crypt on the 1st November every year, remaining there with a guard of honour until the 11th November.

The clearing of the banks of the Meuse made it possible to construct the *quai de Londres* ("London quay," in homage to the Verdun — London committee), in felicitous symmetry with the *quai de la République,* where the *Cercle Militaire* (Officers' Club), built around 1900, bears witness to the bustling military life of times past. The over-all effect of the whole of the *Parc Japiot* is to aerate and, with a flourish of vegetation, to open the way from Verdun towards the east

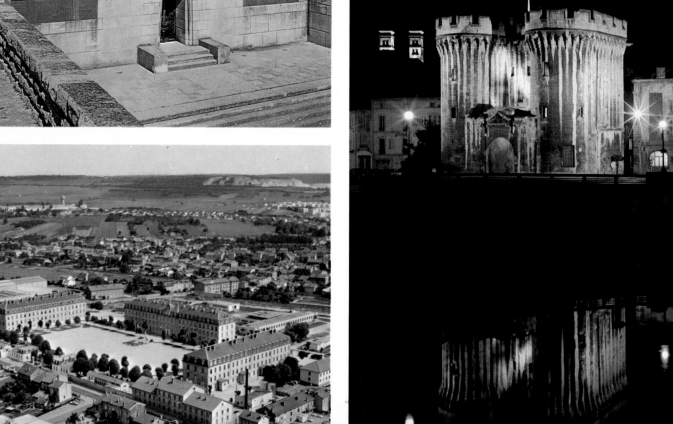

An aerial view of the Parc Japiot with the city centre in the background.

The banks of the Meuse and the Officers' Club.

Above left: the Victory Monument. The crypt housing the golden book of medals won at Verdun is framed by two Russian cannons.

Below left: the barracks of the Miribel quarters.

Above right: The Cercle Militaire (Officers' Club), the Meuse, the bridge and the Tour Chaussée.

Below right: the Porte Chaussée and the Cathedral Towers, illuminated at night.

Historic room in the Underground Citadel. It was here that in 1920 the Unknown Soldier was chosen who now lies under the Arc de Triomphe in Paris. Among the galleries open to the public there is an historical reconstruction (Son et lumière) with more than 70 life-size figures in 8 scenes which depict the life of a French soldier in 1916, as well as reconstructing the historic scenes of the choosing of the Unknown Soldier and the awarding of decorations to the town of Verdun.

and towards the old *Faubourg Pavé* ("Paved Suburb"), where the continuing presence of sternly designed barracks reminds one of the city's traditional rôle.

The Underground Citadel

The period directly after the war was at first characterised by an atmosphere of remembrance, piety and meditation. A moving ceremony seems to denote the beginning of this period: on the 10th November 1920 the unknown soldier subsequently buried at the Arc de Triomphe in Paris was chosen from eight anonymous bodies transferred from all the battlefields to the lower Citadel, at the entrance to the shelter with more then 4 km of galleries excavated from 1888 to 1893. This ritual took place in the presence of the Minister Maginot, who fought at Verdun.

These 4 km of underground passageways were the scene of intense activity during the Great War: apart from 6 gunpowder stores, 7 munitions stores, a siege machine and machines for raising water, 6,000 men could live, rest and work there. This was an unquestionable logistics centre; its bread-ovens worked day and night, sending 28,000 rations daily to the Verdun front. Lastly, a delegation of the Municipal Council, wishing to ensure the permanent presence of the municipality's authorities, stayed in the underground

The Officers' Mess and kitchens of the Underground Citadel.

The dormitories of the Underground Citadel where 6,000 men could be billeted, rest and work.

The Faubourg Pavé *National Cemetery (5,000 graves). In the centre, the square with the 7 unknown soldiers laid to rest there after the selection of the one who symbolises — below the Arc de Triomphe in Paris — the 1,700,000 Frenchmen who fell in the 1914-18 war.*

Citadel throughout the war (the town council had withdrawn to Paris — Rue de Belle Chasse).

If you leave the *Faubourg Pavé,* going towards the battlefield, the military cemetery of *Faubourg Pavé* is preceded by a garden laid out by the *Comité de Verdun du Souvenir Français* ("Verdun Committee of France's Memory"). A monument to those who were shot and executed was erected at the end of the central avenue in 1947, thanks to the talent of Cuvelle it evokes the martyrs and sufferings of all the conflicts. The square of the unknown soldiers (among which the one now resting under the Arc de Triom-

An aerial view of the Douaumont Ossuary, the bodies of 130,000 unknown soldiers; and of the national cemetery, 15,000 graves of identified French soldiers.

phe in Paris was chosen, at the Citadel) is at the centre of the national cemetery, which contains almost 5,000 graves. Near the entrance to the civilian cemetery, which is next to the national cemetery, there is a granite monument in memory of the pioneers of aviation, Nieuport, Thierry de Ville d'Auvray and Bresson, killed in 1911-1912-1913 while on active service. With them, all the airmen who fell at Verdun are commemorated.

A fine wrought iron cross adorns the civilian cemetery. It is by Gauny, of Verdun, who was, according to legend, Louis XVI's master in ironwork. Before the Revolution, this cross stood on the present-day *Pont* (Bridge) *Legay,* previously known as *Pont Sainte Croix* ("Holy Cross Bridge") and *Pont Beaurepaire.*

THE OSSUARY

The Ossuary at Douaumont unites in one resting place the unidentified remains of around 130,000 French and German soldiers collected from the chaotic battlefield, devastated by 51 months of appalling war. The remains were initially placed in coffins bearing the names of the sectors where they had been found, in a provisional Ossuary, a large shed of planks built as early as 1919; today they lie at rest in the monument designed by the architects Azema, Hardy and Edrei. This Ossuary was raised by the initiative of a committee presided over by Monseigneur Ginisty, Bishop of Verdun, who collected the necessary funds by means of subscriptions and lecture tours in France and abroad.

The Ossuary and national cemetery at Douaumont. The dome is a fair reproduction of the cylindrical/conical shape of a shell...

CETTE TOUR A ETE OFFERTE AUX GRANDS MORTS DE VERDUN PAR LEURS AMIS DES ETATS-UNIS

The Ossuary Cloister (137 m. in length) and the 18 alcoves where the tombs are located.

QUI QUE TU SOIS PASSANT ENTRE ET SALUE BIEN BAS
LES RESTES DES HEROS TOMBES POUR TON SALUT

OSSUAIRE DE DOUAUMONT
CHAPELLE PROVISOIRE

The provisional Ossuary built in 1919. In the foreground, the statue of Resignation.

An alcove in the Ossuary Cloister where two granite tombs cover vaults with 14 cubic metres each of remains of unknown soldiers. Above each tomb is the name of the sector where the remains were collected.

One end of the Ossuary Cloister, where a vault of 150 cubic metres was added to accomodate the surplus of remains from the sectors where most men died. It is surmounted by a granite shield where the flame of remembrance is lit on days when services are held.

The Chapel door.

The Poilu *(Private Soldier) of Verdun and the Statue of Silence (by Mme. Girardet).*

The Chapel of Douaumont Ossuary.
Three of the stained glass windows decorating the chapel, by the Master Glassmaker G. Desvallières (1927): Offering of the Wives and Mothers; Stretcher-bearers and male Nurses; The Sacrifice.

The foundation stone was laid on the 22nd August 1920, the remains kept in the provisional Ossuary were transferred in 1927; and the monument, entirely completed, was officially opened on the 7th April 1932. The coats of arms of the towns that contributed to the construction of the Ossuary figure on its façade, which is 137 m. long.

There is a tower 46 m. high in a line with the entrance; its shape resembles that of the shell responsible for the disintegration of the soldiers' bodies, but also bears the cross which gives meaning to all these sacrifices. The tower is surmounted by a lantern of the dead composed of a beacon with four white and red lights around a bell weighing 2,300 kg. Eighteen alcoves have been opened up in the cloister, with two granite tombs in each, donated by towns and departments. Each tomb bears the name of the sector of the battlefield corresponding to the burial vault below, where the remains are gathered together. The surplus of remains from the sectors where most men died made it necessary to add an extra burial vault of 150 cubic metres at each end of the cloister. These two vaults are surmounted by granite shields where the flame of remembrance burns on days when services are held.

The mosaic paving tiles on the Cloister floor represent national military orders: the cross of the Legion of Honour in the centre, the Military Medal at each end and a succession of Croix de Guerre in between. In line with the entrance door is a fine teak door affor-

A back-lit effect over the Douaumont Ossuary and the national cemetery.

The great Victory Bell (2,300 kg) at the top of the Ossuary tower.

ding access to the Catholic chapel, where a moving *Pietà* sculpture above the High Altar welcomes the pilgrim. The stained glass windows depicting scenes of the battle, which were donated by the soldiers' relatives, are by the master glass-maker Desvallières. Monseigneur Ginisty and Canon Noël, founder of the Ossuary project and its first chaplain respectively, chose to lie among the anonymous victims whose tomb they helped to build.

The Ossuary was built on Thiaumont crest; the ruined fort, a few hundred metres to the west, still bears this

German military cemeteries in the Verdun battle sector. (Azanne, Ville devant Chaumont, Hautecourt, Romagne devant Montfaucon).

D

Deutscher Soldatenfriedhof 1914-18

Cimitière Militaire Allemand

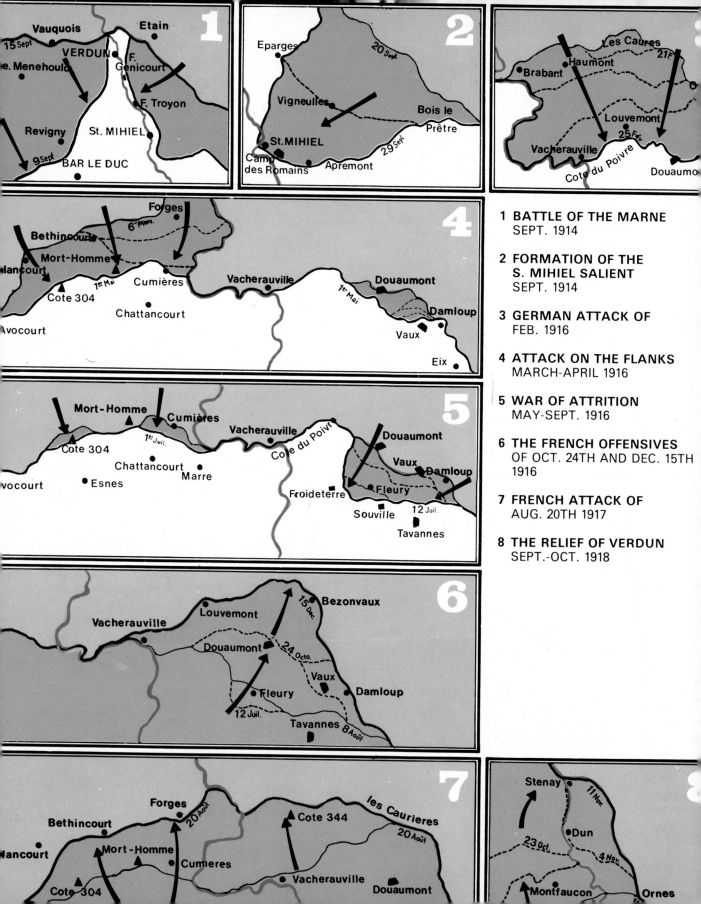

1 BATTLE OF THE MARNE
SEPT. 1914

2 FORMATION OF THE S. MIHIEL SALIENT
SEPT. 1914

3 GERMAN ATTACK OF
FEB. 1916

4 ATTACK ON THE FLANKS
MARCH-APRIL 1916

5 WAR OF ATTRITION
MAY-SEPT. 1916

6 THE FRENCH OFFENSIVES
OF OCT. 24TH AND DEC. 15TH 1916

7 FRENCH ATTACK OF
AUG. 20TH 1917

8 THE RELIEF OF VERDUN
SEPT.-OCT. 1918

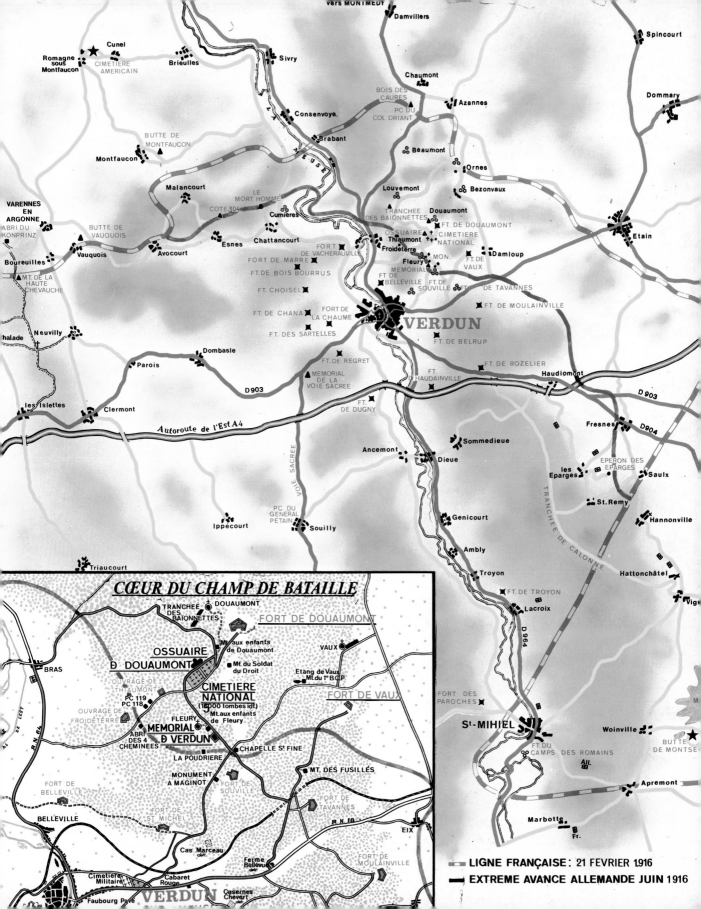

vers MONTMEDY

Spincourt

Damvillers

Cunel
Romagne sous Montfaucon
CIMETIERE AMERICAIN
Brieulles
Sivry
Chaumont
Dommary

Consenvoye
BOIS DES CAURES
PC DU COL DRIANT
Azannes

BUTTE DE MONTFAUCON
Brabant
Beaumont

Montfaucon
Ornes
Etain

VARENNES EN ARGONNE
Malancourt
LE MORT HOMME
COTE 304
Louvemont
Bezonvaux

ABRI DU KONPRINZ
BUTTE DE VAUQUOIS
Cumières
TRANCHEE DES BAIONNETTES
Douaumont
FT. DE DOUAUMONT

Boureuilles
Vauquois
Avocourt
Esnes
Chattancourt
OSSUAIRE
Thiaumont
Froideterre
CIMETIERE NATIONAL
Damloup

FORT DE MARRE
FORT DE VACHERAUVILLE
Fleury
MON.
FT. DE VAUX

MT. DE LA HAUTE CHEVAUCHE
FT. DE BOIS BOURRUS
MEMORIAL
FT DE BELLEVILLE
FT. DE SOUVILLE
FT. DE TAVANNES

chalade
Neuvilly
FT. CHOISEL
FT. DE MOULAINVILLE

FT. DE CHANA
FORT DE LA CHAUME
VERDUN

Dombasle
FT. DES SARTELLES
FT. DE BELRUP

Parois
FT. DE REGRET
FT. DE ROZELIER
Haudiomont

D 903
MEMORIAL DE LA VOIE SACREE
FT. D'HAUDAINVILLE
D 903

les Islettes
Clermont
FT. DE DUGNY
Fresnes
D 904

Autoroute de l'Est A4

Ancemont
Sommedieue
EPERON DES EPARGES

Dieue
les Eparges
Saulx

PC DU GENERAL PETAIN
St. Remy

Ippécourt
Souilly
Genicourt
Hannonville

Ambly

Troyon
FT. DE TROYON
Hattonchâtel

Triaucourt
Lacroix
Vig

FORT DES PAROCHES

St-MIHIEL
Woinville
BUTTE DE MONTSE

FT. DU CAMPS DES ROMAINS
All.

Apremont

Marbotte
Fr.

CŒUR DU CHAMP DE BATAILLE

TRANCHEE DES BAIONNETTES
DOUAUMONT
FORT DE DOUAUMONT

Mt. aux enfants de Douaumont
VAUX

BRAS
OSSUAIRE Ð DOUAUMONT
Mt. du Soldat du Droit

OUVRAGE DE THIAUMONT
CIMETIERE NATIONAL
(16000 tombes idl.)
Etang de Vaux
Mt. du 1° BCP
FORT DE VAUX

PC 119
PC 118
Mt. aux enfants de Fleury

OUVRAGE DE FROIDÉTERRE
FLEURY
MEMORIAL Ð VERDUN

ABRI DES 4 CHEMINEES
CHAPELLE St FINE

LA POUDRIERE
MONUMENT A MAGINOT
FORT DE SOUVILLE
MT. DES FUSILLÉS

FORT DE BELLEVILLE
FORT DE ST MICHEL
FORT DE TAVANNES

BELLEVILLE
R.N. 18
EIX
FORT DE MOULAINVILLE

Cas. Marceau

Ferme Bellevue
Cimetiere Militaire
Cabaret Rouge

VERDUN
Caserne Chevert
Faubourg Pavé

▬▬▬ LIGNE FRANÇAISE : 21 FEVRIER 1916

▬▬▬ EXTREME AVANCE ALLEMANDE JUIN 1916

Butte de Vauqois
Of the 13 craters that litter the main street of the destroyed village, the deepest one was caused by the largest German mine (70 tonnes of explosives) on the 16th May 1916, killing 108 French soldiers of the 46th Infantry Regiment and the occupants of the German front line.

(1) Shell-holes dotting the main street of the devastated village.
(2) German front lines.
(3) French front lines.

name. By its side, one may make reverence before the wall/monument to the Jewish volunteers who died for France; its façade is adorned with Biblical passages engraved in Hebrew characters.

Douaumont military cemetery — comprising 15,000 graves — slopes gently down in front of the Ossuary. Each grave is marked by a white cross, except those of Moslem soldiers, which are surmounted by a stele orientated towards Mecca. Many of their German comrades killed before Verdun also repose in lands of the Meuse: there are 54,845 identified bodies distributed in 29 German national cemeteries within what was the Verdun battle sector. The *Réconciliation par dessus les tombes* ("Reconciliation above the graves") Association, which is composed of young French and German people, meets regularly for summer camps around these necropolises, which it also helps to maintain.

VAUQUOIS - LES EPARGES

The high areas of Vauquois, in Argonne, and Les Eparges, in the *Hauts de Meuse,* were sectors that had been particularly fiercely disputed in 1914 and 1915, before the February 1916 attack on Verdun. Mines made their début here and the holes, still clearly visible like so many dead craters, speak eloquently of the extent of the underground works where French

Vauquois: The Monument built on the site of the old town hall (architect Monestier, sculptor Roussel).

Les Eparges: Point X Monument, dedicated to the 10,000 men who disappeared in the clay of the hill (sculptor Fischer).

Monument to the Ghosts of the 106th Infantry Regiment (by Maxime Del Sarte).

sappers and German pioneers loaded blast-holes with tens of tons of explosives at a time.

A simple shelling attack caused Vauquois to fall to the Germans on the 24th September. The rounded gaize hillock of Vauquois, with a height of 295 m. above sea-level, 130 m. above the valleys of the Aire and the Buanthe, was an important observation point to reoccupy. The first attempts, in October and December 1914, ended in failure. The battles of the *Butte* (Hillock) *de Vauqois* that have become legendary took place in February and March 1915. The knoll was literally torn to shreds by the explosions of mines and large-calibre shells. The hill's definitive recapture, in March 1915, caused a heavy toll of deaths. The village standing on the top was completely pulverized. The monument that has been built there, on the site of the old town hall, is a pyramid (architect Monestier, sculptor Roussel) guarded by a soldier in the uniform of 1915, on the point of throwing a grenade.

From the 21st September 1914 onwards the Germans had occupied Les Eparges plateau, 1400 m. long, between the villages of Combres and Les Eparges, dominating the Woëvre plain to the east of the hills of the Meuse. As at Vauquois, they had converted this ridge into a very powerfully fortified stronghold. Reoccupying the higher positions cost the French considerable attacks and unheard-of efforts. The first assault was from the 17th to the 19th February 1915. It was preceded by the detonation of mines and allowed our troops to gain the Germans' front line. The French suffered furious counter-attacks but were able to maintain their positions by means of inhuman efforts (the 106th Infantry Regiment lost 1,600 men: 300 killed, 1,000 wounded and 300 lost without trace). On the 18th, 19th and 27th March, murderous partial attacks enabled us to approach the goal more; the assaults of the 5th, 6th and 9th April secured the definitive conquest of the west ridge, opposite Les

Spur of Les Eparges: The Germans captured this remarkable observation post on the 21st September 1914. The struggle became a war of mines, causing enormous craters. Hand-to-hand fighting was the order of the day. The French took the position again on the 10th April 1915.

(1) Point X.
(2) German lines.
(3) French lines.
(4) Point C.
(5) Shell-holes.

Eparges. The conquest of Point X — opposite the Woëvre — necessitated successive attacks and counter-attacks up to October 1915. The men fought with grenades in an intolerable atmosphere of putrefaction, under incessant shelling. The losses were terrible: on the 10th April 1915 the 25th B.C.P. left 474 men on the battle-ground and two days later the 67th Infantry Regiment had lost a total of 1,029 men.

Three monuments stand nearby the line of enormous craters caused by the explosions. The one designated ''of Point X'', dedicated to the 10,000 men who disappeared in the clay of the hill, was sculptured by Fischer (it is near the Memorial to the *anciens du*

Génie, or technicians); the one in the middle (by Lefebvre-Klein, called the *Monument du Coq,* or monument of the cock) commemorates the sacrifices of the 12th Infantry Division; and the monument called *des Revenants du 106° Régiment d'Infanterie* (of the 106th Infantry Regiment's Ghosts), to the west, is the work of Maxime Real del Sarte. The area of Les Eparges, as also Vauquois, has been cleared and is maintained by the *Association Nationale du Souvenir de la Bataille de Verdun* (National Association in Memory of the Battle of Verdun), with the help of the Army and the National Forests Department. Maps and a tape-recording enable one to situate and understand the events better.

The Verdun Battle Memorial/Museum (1914-1918), located on the site of the old station at Fleury.

THE BATTLE OF VERDUN

21st February - 15th December 1916

Summary of Events

In September 1914 Verdun was the eastern bastion where the right flank of the French Army, fighting in the Marne, was entrenched. The fortress was cleared on the 9th September and maintained its salient position, but the decree of the 5th August 1915 degraded it and integrated the fortress to the greater whole of the Fortified Region of Verdun, which stretched from Avocourt, in the west, to Saint-Mihiel in the southeast.

Notwithstanding the appearances, the decision to attack Verdun in particular implied considerable advantages for the Germans. Apart from the numerous communications systems at their disposal in the Woëvre (Verdun had only the weak umbilical cord of the Bar-le-Duc road and a narrow-gauge railway), by attacking from the north Falkenhayn hoped to oblige his enemy to evacuate the right bank of the Meuse, or else to defend the outpost by constantly supplying the battle with fresh troops, destined to be rapidly exhausted. The frontal attack was launched on the 21st February 1916 and finished at the beginning of March.

An enormous stock of artillery, accumulated around

A French 520 mm shell. *A French 400 mm shell.* *A German 420 mm shell.*

French and German armaments used in the 1914-1918 war, on show at the entrance to the Fleury Memorial.

Verdun over a period of months, enabled the Germans to launch a preliminary bombardment at 7.15 a.m. on the 21st February. This shelling by about 3,000 guns of all calibres *(Trommelfeuer)* ended at 4.00 p.m., leaving the assault troops to attack on a front 10 km long, between Brabant and Ornes. Three army corps made substantial north-south advances at first, then came up against the débris of the units in the sector, who resisted them fiercely. Among these were Colonel Driant's 1,300 riflemen, in Les Caures wood, of whom only a hundred survivors returned. The attackers were surprised by this unexpected resistance, and they renewed the infernal shelling. Despite their slowing the progression, and desperate defence, the French troops' situation deteriorated: Brabant fell on the 23rd; and on the 24th the

defenders, having lost 50% of the total strength deployed in a few days (20,000 men), were exhausted despite the hasty reinforcements thrown into the furnace after arriving by forced march. The Fort of Douaumont was occupied without a struggle on the 25th. That same night General de Castelnau, sent urgently by Joffre, decided to maintain the defence on the right bank and General Pétain — who installed his H.Q. at Souilly — was charged with directing operations from the 26th onwards. Pétain immediately had the forts still held by the French rearmed; he reorganized the chaotic battle-field and restored confidence to the men and officers engaged in the ordeal. The German attack was checked by the 28th, although it continued until the 5th March. Their attempt at a frontal break having failed, the Germans

*A German
380 mm shell.*

*Above: a 105 mm gun, 1913 model.
Below: a heavy 240 mm trench-mortar.*

A 170 mm Minenwerfer. ▷

modified their plans and tried to wear the French battle corps down by attracting as many divisions as possible to the area before Verdun in the hope that this strangulated position as an outpost beyond the lines, so damaging for our communications, would neither allow us to relieve the units before they were annihilated, nor to supply them with reinforcements and provisions. But the organization of the *Voie Sacrée* ("the Holy Path"), making possible the prompt rotation of the French divisions on the battlefield before they were completely exhausted, frustrated this plan. Be that as it may, the Germans broadened their front by 20 km from the 6th March onwards, extending it as far as Avocourt on the left bank.

Thenceforth the attacks alternated on either bank.

Inside the Fleury Memorial, with the fighter planes, the reconstruction of the terrain with trenches and dug-outs, and the large illuminated map which enables visitors to grasp the essential strategical phases of the assault on Verdun.

The principal battles on the left bank were those of Mort-Homme and *Cote* (Hill) 304; on the right bank the main thrusts were on the Vaux-Thiaumont-Fleury-Souville axis. The village of Vaux was lost, and its fort menaced, on the 2nd April. Then, on the 9th April, the Germans launched a general offensive on both banks. Notwithstanding their courage and the dense shelling, the defenders' tenacity was no lesser and this offensive failed. Geographically more limited — but just as fierce — attacks were subsequently engaged. The Mangin unit made an unsuccessful attempt to recapture Douaumont fort in May, and the one at Vaux fell on the 7th June. From the 23rd June to the 12th July the Germans tried a massive last offensive, throwing 17 regiments towards Froideterre-Fleury-Souville. The French and British troops, however, were attacking in the Somme as from the 1st July, and the Germans lost the initiative in the Verdun area. The violence in the localised struggles nevertheless continued throughout the summer, it centred particularly on the Thiaumont-Fleury-Chapelle-Sainte-Fine-Souville-Vaux-Douaumont "quadrilateral." Every inch of terrain was disputed with incredible ferocity. Whole days of battle were needed to win a few metres of land: Fleury and the fortifications at Thiaumont were captured over and again; the headquarters posts of *La Poudrière, Les Quatre Cheminées* and P.C. 118-119 were the centre of extremely violent struggles where the combattants' courage and abnegation were incomparable (the German losses were so great that their reserve regiments were advanced to the battle-front on the 25th June).

La Boue ("The Mud"), a striking model, by Alphonse Prévost, exhibited in the Memorial at Fleury devant Douaumont.

The Memorial at Fleury-devant-Douaumont: a detail of the rconstruction of the havoc of the battlefield.

Vers l'Oubli ("Towards Oblivion"): a reconstruction of Pouzargues' painting.

But General Nivelle — who succeeded General Pétain on the 1st May, the latter was appointed Commander-in-Chief of the 2nd Army — was able to prepare a counter-attack in order to clear the advanced positions. In October and November 1916, General Mangin launched an offensive towards the northeast, with solid logistical support and considerable artillery backing. The Moroccan Colonial Infantry Regiment recaptured Douaumont fort on the 24th October; and on the 2nd November the fort at Vaux was taken again. On the 15th December 1916 this immense effort was completed by an attack which forced the Germans back to more than 5 km from

Souville, which they had still been threatening in July. The positions of February 1916 were occupied again in August 1917; and finally, in September 1918 the young American army's troops swept the Germans completely away from Verdun, towards Montfaucon in the north.

THE MUSEUM/MEMORIAL OF THE BATTLE OF VERDUN

The Fleury Memorial before Douaumont takes the visitor into another dimension of his pilgrimage. The first thing here is an explanation of the Battle by

△ *Uniforms of French and German artillerymen in 1916.*

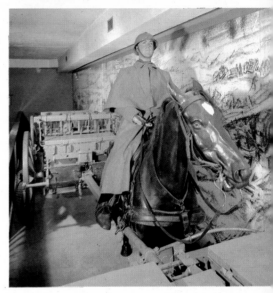

A French artilleryman at Verdun. ▷

A 75 mm gun and its carriage. ▷ ▷

The Memorial at Fleury-devant-Douaumont: the famous
Berliet lorry of the Voie Sacrée ("Holy Path").

Aerial view of the Memorial.

A German look-out man's equipment; German stores.

means of a striking reconstruction of the reality of a
trench with wrecked dug-outs, shell-holes, etc... In
the vestibule preceding the vast main hall one is met
by photographs of the anguished faces of a French in-
fantryman and his German adversary; inside, precise
information about conditions in the battle, seen and
explained from both sides, is distributed right around
the hall: documents, maps, diverse material from cannons to aeroplanes including the famous lorry of the
Voie Sacrée, guns, uniforms and portraits. An illuminated mural map makes it possible to understand
in a few minutes the essential strategical phases of
the attack before Verdun.

The Memorial is a private work erected by the
devoutness of the ex-service men in homage to their
dead. It was opened in 1967 and the collections have
been unceasingly enriched since then, just as its fame
has augmented. Almost 250,000 people visit it every
year, as one of the essential poles of cultural tourism
in Verdun. This is not its only activity. The organization which promoted the construction of the
Memorial, the Comité National du Souvenir de la
Bataille de Verdun — whose Honorary Chairman was
Maurice Génevoix (the author of Ceux de 14) until his
death in 1980 — and a local delegation, the Association Nationale du Souvenir de la Bataille de Verdun,
have their headquarters there. With its various com-
missions (Studies, Information, History, Public Rela-
tions), the Association concerns itself with restoring
the battlefield and, by means of publications and

VILLAGE DÉTRUIT de FLEURY-DEVANT-DOUAUMONT

The Chapel and Statue of Our Lady of Europe (sculptor A. Forfert).

Fleury-devant-Douaumont: one of the nine villages that were never rebuilt. The ground was so affected by the arms, scrap and human remains that all traces of habitation and vegetation disappeared. As in the greater part of the "red zone," the village — which has been

studies, making the young generations understand the sacrifice of the soldiers at Verdun, and the moral that may be drawn from their sufferings, which nobody prevented.

FLEURY

The Memorial has been built on the site of Fleury's little station where, until 1914, a narrow-gauge train used to stop: *le meusien.* The village itself was a few paces from there, it had more than 400 inhabitants who grew cereals and worked in the woods. A stone inscription by the roadside reminds the visitor that there was once a village here, destroyed just as eight others in the Verdun battle sector were completely wiped off the map. Fleury, furthermore, was located in the heart of the quadrilateral where the battle was particularly fierce. The village was in the hands of the French — and pulverized by the German artillery — until June 1916. It was in the course of the Germans' desperate efforts to occupy the position, then in the continued struggles for possession of the ridge, that the village — or what was left of it — was the cause of atrocious combats. It was the last key blocking all advance towards Verdun. In this period Fleury changed hands 16 times. The French and Germans lived the same hell, dug in a few metres from one another, fighting with identical courage and bitterness. The village fell on the 11th July and was recaptured by the Moroccan tirailleurs on the 17th-18th August. The French nation has not wished Fleury to remain invisible for perpetuity, like the other villages that disappeared in the "red zone." It still exists legally: it has a mayor. Those who once lived there and their descendants meet up every year at the little chapel that was built after the war. A statue of Our Lady of Europe was unveiled on the chapel's main front in 1979. By initiative of the A.N.S.B.V. and with the help of the *Equipement* and the National Forests Department, the village's ground-plan has been restored and marked out so that the visitor may tread in the footsteps of those who had to leave this corner of land...

symbolically recreated — is now covered by woodland. By following the course of what were once the village streets, one can still perceive how the area was devastated.

RUE DE L'EGLISE

Aerial view of Douaumont Fort, and the zone of the German attack of the 21st-25th February 1916.

(1) Caures wood. (2) Herbebois. (3) La Wavrille. (4) The German attack. (5) Observation posts. (6) Machine-gun turret. (7) 75 mm. turret. (8) Bourges casemate. (9) Moat. (10) Double counter-escarpment casing. (11) 155 mm. turret. (12) Interior courtyard. (13) Normal entrance.

Zigzags in an interior gallery.

Aerial photograph taken directly over the Fort.

Bourges casemate.

DOUAUMONT FORT

Douaumont fort, at Hill 388, was built from 1885 onwards and constantly fortified until 1913; it is first and foremost an excellent observation post. The installations are amongst the most imposing in all the ring of fortifications around Verdun: the fort is equipped with flanking parapets, concrete casemates (special concrete shell 2.50 m. thick), a 155 R turret, a 75 turret and two machine-gun turrets. The Germans considered Douaumont to be the essential key to the system of fortifications. Unfortunately it did not fulfil its expected part in the events of 1916. Indeed, in the course of a general revision of the fortifications in August 1915, it was degraded and its supplies partly removed in favour of the active troops. The artillery remained in place but the fort had a garrison of only 57 territorials when, on the 25th February, the German advance brought up a company of the 24th Brandenburg Infantry Regiment to occupy it without a fight. After an abortive attempt on the 22nd May, it was recaptured by the Moroccan Colonial Infantry Regiment on the 24th October 1916.

During the whole of the Germans' occupation, they organized Douaumont as a shelter for passing troops and a logistical base. They furthermore enjoyed excellent views which enabled them to direct the attacks towards Fleury and Souville, particularly in June and July.

At the time of their taking the fort, it was practically intact despite violent shelling by large-calibre artillery from the 21st to the 25th February. From the 26th February onwards it underwent daily bombardment by the French with shells ranging from 155 to 400 mm in calibre. When the fort was recaptured, and notwithstanding the amazing quantity of projectiles that had fallen on the superstructure and the effect of vibrations, the concrete shell had withstood everything due to its mass and probably also thanks to the layer of sand placed between the concrete and the masonry vaults. The Germans suffered intensely from the lack of water, non-existent ventilation, echo and resonance of explosions: a severe test for their nerves. Further, the accidental detonation of a stock of grenades on the 8th May caused heavy losses among the troops stationed in the barracks. The 679 victims were interred in a walled gallery marked by a chapel where German ex-service men come to meditate.

Wartime barracks.

Douaumont Fort: interior courtyard and the protective fortifications.

Panoramic view of the west front: (below) interior courtyard.

Douaumont Fort: French chapel.

Casemate.

The German chapel, marking the site where the 679 victims of the explosion of a store of grenades (8th May 1916) were buried (above).

"Wasserkeller": a casemate serving as washroom.

Christ carved on a wall by a German soldier.

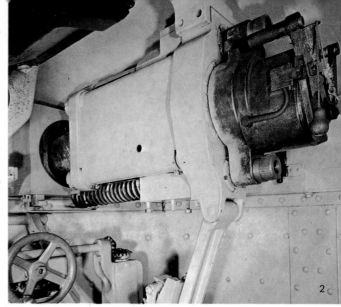

1. Douaumont Fort's fortifications: superstructure of the 75 turret and the observation post.

2. Gun-chamber.

3. The underground part of the 75 turret seen from inside the fort.

4. Rotating trench gun, 1879 model.

5. The Observation Post and one of the two machine-gun turrets on the Fort's superstructure.

6. The underground part of the machine-gun turret.

7. The superstructure of the 155 turret.

8. The underground part of the 155 turret.

The commemorative tablet devoted to the defenders of Vaux Fort.

The commemorative tablet evoking the last pigeon.

DON DES MEMBRES DE L'ASSOCIATION
"LES DÉFENSEVRS DU"
FORT DE VAVX

DANS CE FORT EN RUINES 250 HOMMES RÉSISTÈRENT PENDANT SEPT JOURS (DU 1ᵉʳ AU 7 JUIN 1916) AUX ASSAUTS FURIEUX DES ALLEMANDS, AUX ATTAQUES PAR GAZ ET LIQUIDES ENFLAMMÉS, AUX TORTURES DE LA SOIF.

LA GARNISON ÉTAIT CONSTITUÉE PAR DES ÉLÉMENTS DES UNITÉS SUIVANTES : 6ᵐᵉ ET 7ᵐᵉ Cⁱᵉ DU 142ᵐᵉ R.I. LES 3ᵐᵉˢ Cⁱᵉˢ DE MITRAILLEURS DU 142ᵐᵉ ET 53ᵐᵉ R.I. DÉTACHEMENTS DU GÉNIE SAPEURS DU 2ᵐᵉ RÉGᵗ ET 9ᵐᵉ Rᵗ. DÉTᵐᵉⁿᵗˢ D'ARTILLERIE DU 5ᵐᵉ R.A.P ET 6ᵐᵉ R.A. POSTE DE SECOURS DU 101ᵐᵉ R.I.

TEXTE OFFICIEL DE LA REDDITION DU FORT
AUX CONDITIONS SUIVANTES :
AVEC LES HONNEURS DE LA GUERRE, TRAITEMENTS AVEC ÉGARDS, FACULTÉ LAISSÉE AUX OFFICIERS D'EMMENER LEUR ORDONNANCE. OBJETS PERSONNELS LAISSÉS AUX POSSESSEURS.
JE REMETS LES LOCAUX ET PARTIES D'OUVRAGE ENCORE EN MON POUVOIR DANS LE FORT DE VAUX AUX TROUPES ALLEMANDES
FORT DE VAUX LE 7 JUIN 1916
LE CHEF DE BATAILLON COMMANDANT LE FORT
RAYNAL

1916
1914   1929

AVX COLOMBOPHILES
MORTS POVR LA FRANCE
AV PIGEON DE VERDVN

DE CE FORT EST PARTI PENDANT LA BATAILLE
VERDUN, LE 4 JUIN 1916, LE DERNIER PIG
VOYAGEUR DU COMMANDANT RAYNAL (N°78
PORTANT LE MESSAGE SUIVANT :

" NOUS TENONS TOUJOURS, MAIS NOUS SUBISSONS U
ATTAQUE, PAR LES GAZ ET LES FUMÉES, TRÈS DANGEREU
IL Y A URGENCE À NOUS DÉGAGER. FAITES-NOUS DONNER DE SU
COMMUNICATION OPTIQUE PAR SOUVILLE QUI NE RÉPOND F
A NOS APPELS. C'EST MON DERNIER PIGEON "

LE PIGEON ACCOMPLIT SA MISSION ET A OBT
LA CITATION SUIVANTE :

" MALGRÉ DES DIFFICULTÉS ÉNORMES RÉSULTANT D'UNE INTEN
FUMÉE ET D'UNE ÉMISSION ABONDANTE DE GAZ, A ACCOMPLI LA MISS
DONT L'AVAIT CHARGÉ LE COMMANDANT RAYNAL UNIQUE MOY
DE COMMUNICATION DE L'HÉROÏQUE DÉFENSEUR DU FORT DE VAUX
TRANSMIS LES DERNIERS RENSEIGNEMENTS QUI AIENT ÉTÉ REÇ
DE CET OFFICIER. FORTEMENT INTOXIQUÉ EST ARRIVÉ MOURA
AU COLOMBIER.

Diplôme de Bacue d'Honneu

CETTE PLAQUE A ÉTÉ ÉRIGÉE PAR SOUSCRIPTION DES SOCIÉTÉS COLOMBOPHIL

VAUX FORT

The fort at Vaux, the north-east bastion of Verdun's permanent fortifications, was built from 1881 to 1884 and reinforced in 1888 so as to take into account the progress made in explosives. In 1904-06, it was equipped with a 75 mm turret and observatory, three counterscarp parapets and two casemates armed with two 75 mm guns. Unfortunately the fort suffered the consequences of the August 1915 decree which also withdrew the garrison from Douaumont. On the 26th February 1916, the mined turret exploded under the impact of a German shell. On the same day, General Pétain — assuming command at Souilly and conscious of these forts' interest — might well order them to be reoccupied for Vaux was no more than a fort without arms which a hastily assembled garrison set about defending. After taking Douaumont the Germans, constrained to broaden their front, came up against Vaux. It was attacked from the 5th to the 30th March and the village fell on the 2nd April. The fort itself had resisted well, although the shelling was intense. On the 1st June, after very hard fighting in which the lack of support by its neighbour Douaumont on the flank was cruelly apparent, it was outflanked to the north-east and hemmed in on three sides. The wavering building, like a ship lost in the storm, was boarded on the superstructure on the 2nd June. For five days there was hand-to-hand fighting — in which the only match for the assailants' audacity was the stubborn heroism of the little garrison led by Major Raynal — in the passage-ways which were encumbered by the wounded, stifled with smoke and gas, set ablaze by flame-throwers and resounding with the din of explosions. Thirst alone determined this formidable savageness: the cisterns were empty,

Vaux Fort: the Dovecote and the Telephone Exchange.

Vaux Fort: the Chapel.

A grave.

A sick room.

fissured by the shelling. The exhausted garrison had to surrender but not before the commanding officer, by a supreme effort, had been able to evacuate about a hundred men in the night of the 5th to the 6th and had communicated the tragic nature of the situation by sending his last carrier-pigeon on the 4th June. The men of the Vaux fort received the honours of war from their conquerors. When the fort was abandoned by the Germans on the 2nd November 1916, the French, who were then only 350 m. away, immediately reoccupied it.

Major Raynal's Command Post.

Vaux Fort:
Inside the Bourges casemate, armed with a 75 mm gun.

The observation post and 75 turret destroyed on the 26th February 1916.

A casemate.

FROIDETERRE - THIAUMONT - SOUVILLE - QUATRE CHEMINEES - LA POUDRIERE

Once in possession of Douaumont and Vaux, the two fundamental bases, the Germans were in a position to launch fierce offensives against the last ridges separating them from Verdun, marked by Froideterre, Thiaumont and Souville. The most violent combats took place in this narrow sector of the battlefield, and it was here that the soldiers' suffering, heroism and sense of sacrifice and duty attained such levels that their memory still resounds today in these high places. It was the summer of 1916. Heat and thirst were added to the shells, machine-guns, grenades and flame-throwers, transforming the slightest casualty into a person ravaged by fever and pain. The soldiers of Verdun — under cover in their shell-holes or in the slightest haven from the sun, isolated, a few metres from the enemy who was living the same nightmare — held out by will-power, morale and by the comradeship in arms which sometimes helped them to live, more often to die, but always to suffer. In June 1916, the attackers made a great effort to outflank the last French position. Time was short: the German command knew that an Anglo-French offensive was about to be launched in the Somme. The supreme assault was on the 23rd June after two days of intense preparation by artillery (including gas-shells). The Germans hoped to enter Verdun on the

An aerial view of the fortress and hill at Froideterre. This fortress lies on the axis of a ridge with a series of fortified elements: Quatre-Cheminées, P.C. 118-119, Thiaumont, Douaumont; the last natural obstacle before the Meuse valley and Verdun.

(1) Observation post. (2) Machine-gun turret. (3) 75 mm. turret. (4) Barracks. (5) Bourges casemate. (6) Ossuary. (7) Interior courtyard.

25th. They threw 19 regiments forward on a front 6 km long, appearing out of all the gullies leading to Froideterre, Fleury and Souville. Thiaumont fell, then Fleury. At the end of June, the situation was uncertain. On the 11th and 12th July, in a last effort, the waves of German assaults appropriated Sainte-Fine crossroads in an impressive onslaught and climbed on to the superstructure of Souville fort but here — in view of Verdun, only a few kilometres away, for their foremost units could distinguish the Cathedral towers through the smoke — they were unable to push the attack through and were definitively halted. The wounded lion, the 130th Division's monument with the numbers of all the divisions that fought in this sec-

tor engraved on its plinth, marks this end-point of the German offensive. It is a few metres from Sainte-Fine crossroads, where there were ruins of a little chapel — dependant on the village of Fleury — before 1914, which was the object of a local pilgrimage until the start of the 20th century.

In 1915, units stationed in this sector had raised the walls of the little haven of peace, and military chaplains held mass there.

The ruins of Souville fort, covered with undergrowth, lie at a short distance from the crossroads. The A.N.S.B.V. has uncovered a curious steel casemate destined to house two machine-guns: the Pamard casemate. The rest of the fortifications are inaccessi-

The Wounded Lion Monument at the Chapelle Sainte-Fine crossroads marks the extreme point reached by the German advance.

Aerial view of what was once Souville Fort. One may discern the Pamard casemate which it was possible to clear.

The Maginot Monument, west of Souville Fort.

ble. They were very severely damaged because the fort was built from 1875 to 1881, on the standard plan for masonry fortifications, and when Vaux and Douaumont were built it became a second-line defence and was thus not reinforced. It was nevertheless equipped with a double 155 turret in 1890-91, this did not give satisfaction and was taken out of service on the 10th April 1916; it was not restored until 1917. Despite being out of date, and despite the intense shelling (from the 21st April to the 21st June it was struck by 38,000 shells, a number of them 380 and 420 calibre) the fort valiantly fulfilled its rôle. From July to October, when the Mangin attack made possible the recapture of Douaumont, the Sainte-Fine Chapel crossroads remained a crucial point in the Battle.

The Maginot Monument stands to the west of Souville fort. André Maginot was elected Deputy for Bar le Duc in 1910. He enlisted voluntarily in 1914 and was posted to the 44th Territorial which was composed almost entirely of *Meusiens* (inhabitants of the Meuse area). At the front from the 11th August 1914 onwards, he formed a corps of voluntary patrollers. André Maginot was wounded and disabled in an engagement in Woëvre, beyond Douaumont, on the 9th November 1914. He occupied his seat in Parliament again in 1916 and was Deputy for the Meuse area until 1932. He was War Minister and gave his name to the concept of the line of fortifications erected along the Rhine frontier as far as Belgium, from 1930 to 1940. His friends and comrades had this monument raised in his memory; it is by Gaston Broquet, the sculptor, and its symbolism is evident: the shield evokes patriotic firmness and the wall recalls the idea of fortification. The visitor will notice that the bronze group, dressed in 1915 uniforms, is also an engaging image of soldiers' comradeship.

Thiaumont fort, command posts 118 and 119, Froideterre and the Quatre Cheminées dug-out

P.C. 118.
Thiaumont: cupola/observation post.
The Fleury Poudrière ("Powder-store").

The south front of Thiaumont fortress.

Aerial view of P.C. 119 (in the background, Douaumont Ossuary and Fort).

The Pamard casemate at Souville Fort (steel casemate for two machine-guns).

received their severest test during the attacks of May and July 1916. In fact these fortifications mark a ridge running from Douaumont towards the south-east and the heights of Belleville, the last natural rampart before the Meuse valley and Verdun. Furthermore, the occupation of this backbone not only afforded observation posts over the left bank, but also — by its flanking position — made it possible to prevent attackers from advancing out of the village of Fleury. All this explains the violence of the attacks towards Froideterre on the 23rd June, which got stranded in the fort's inner courtyard. Thiaumont was a small, intermediate post connecting Douaumont with Froideterre. Although a simple cube of concrete and masonry (the layer of concrete collapsed under the shelling), it was nonetheless equipped with a Bourges casemate housing two 75 guns, machine-guns and an observation post. Its location enabled its garrison to prevent any serious advance on Fleury. As for command posts 118 and 119, they were originally no more than ordinary dug-outs and stores without any heavy guns. They were strengthened with reinforced concrete and captured in the heat of the battle: events made them become defensive centres, hastily fitted with machine-guns and defended by the troops in the sector.

The dug-out at Quatre Cheminées and the Fleury *Poudrière* (Powder-store) were different in conception. Rather than being built on a ridge, for dominating and observing, they were dug against the slope of the rock following a very simple plan of vaulted, carefully faced galleries. The powder-store was one of many depots used to receive and stock shells, gunpowder and big gun cartridges near the forts. Here again, the events converted them into defensive centres, but more particularly shelters for the wounded and front-line command posts.

A communication trench 2 km long led south from the *Poudrière* to Marceau barracks; and Quatre

Quatre Cheminées dug-out, situated under the rock, used as Brigade Command Post and Relief Post during the battle. On the 23rd June 1916 it was on the point of being taken by a Bavarian unit — who already had the superstructure and were throwing grenades down the ventilation shafts — when it was relieved by the 114th Batallion of chasseurs (mountain light infantry) in a vigorous counter-attack.

Cheminées gave directly onto the *Ravin des Vignes* ("Vine Gully") where at night the stretcher-bearers and volunteer American ambulancemen evacuated the wounded, piled up in these overcrowded galleries thick with gas and smoke, towards Bras.

On the 23rd June the fort at Froideterre played the same rôle of stopping the enemy attack as did Souville, to the east, on the 12th July. Froideterre, however, did not have the same potent defensive means as the stronghold at Souville. It was an intermediate fort, built in 1887-88 and completed from 1902 to 1905; it had only a concrete barracks, a Bourges casemate on the west flank towards Charny fort, a 75 turret to the east towards Thiaumont and

two machine-gun turrets. These different elements did not, unfortunately, have any underground communication between them; but the two armoured observation points afforded remarkable views. The Germans reached the gorge in front of the fort on the morning of the 23rd June. In spite of the avalanche of shells directed against the superstructure, particularly in the previous two days, the turrets functioned and the fire from them halted the assailants.

(Froideterre has been cleared by the A.N.S.B.V. with the help of the Army, and restored to a state such that it may be visited freely; so also have command posts 118 and 119, Quatre Cheminées, Thiaumont and the *Poudrière.*)

The Tranchée des Baïonnettes *("Bayonet Trench") where history eventually merged with legend...*

BAYONET TRENCH

History intermingles with legend concerning the *Tranchée des Baïonnettes.* On the 12th June 1916 this entrenched position was a part of the terrain forming a salient west of Douaumont which the Germans wanted to take before launching their main offensive on the 23rd. Two batallions of the 137th Infantry Regiment, who had been at the front since the 10th June, were the object of appalling shelling and very soon found themselves cut off. The men of the 137th were very likely buried alive as was, alas, frequent; others, killed by gas, lay in the trench and their rifles remained leaning against its sides. The Germans over-

Bois *(Wood)* des Caures.

Colonel Driant's grave.

Colonel Driant's Command Post and shelter.

Memorial to Colonel Driant and his infantrymen.

Memorial to the Voie Sacrée.

General Pétain at Souilly Command Post.

Succession of lorries on the Voie Sacrée.

ran the position and finally filled in this mass grave. The Colonel of the 137th had a small wooden monument erected there in January 1919. A generous American patron, Rand, set out the present-day avenue ending at the road in a fine wrought iron gate. This monument was opened by Alexandre Millerand, President of the Republic, in the presence of the ambassador of the United States, on the 8th December 1920.

BOIS DES CAURES

The 56th and 59th B.C.P. of Colonel Driant (Deputy for Nancy and author of the draft bill which instituted the Croix de Guerre), in Les Caures wood, were among the first to be hit by the German attack of the 21st February 1916. The colonel defended his position with a handful of survivors but fell on the 22nd. He was buried under the mausoleum (sculptor G. Calvet) built in 1922 by a committee of ex-riflemen presided over by General de Castelnau.

THE "HOLY PATH"

Only one lung existed to supply this gigantic battle that was being engaged: the secondary road from Bar le Duc to Verdun, which the writer Maurice Barrès was to name *La Voie Sacrée.* One vehicle followed another every 14 seconds in each direction, night and day, over 75 km. This noria, which the soldiers called the "turnstile", transported 90,000 men and 50,000 tons of materials and supplies every week. In ten months, the territorials distributed all along the road

The Monument at Cote (Hill) 304 (Architect Amelin, Sculptor Albert Lance).

The Skeleton Monument at Mort-Homme (Sculptor Froment-Meurice).

threw 700,000 tons of stones under the wheels of the lorries driven by long-suffering drivers consumed by insomnia, burned out by fatigue and harried by the cold. A monument to these anonymous drivers has been erected at the end of the "Holy Path," at the crossroads with the Paris road. The road passes in front of Souilly town hall 20 km from Verdun, where General Pétain and his staff directed the battle from the 26th February to the 1st May 1916.

MORT-HOMME — HILL 304

In the absence of any important fortification systems, the combats on the west bank centred essentially around the high points, authentic natural obstacles, whose possession was indispensable for any progress towards Verdun.

Mort-Homme ("Dead Man") is the name of an ancient location, it is in fact made up of three hills with altitudes of 295 and 265 m. It was fiercely attacked from the 5th March onwards and the Germans occupied the north-west slopes on the 14th. On the 9th April, Mort-Homme was once again the centre of a broad offensive which also included the right bank. There was dreadful hand-to-hand fighting, and the position's central summit was so pounded by the opposing artillery forces that it could no longer be occupied by either side. The Germans nevertheless in-

The Haute Chevauchée Monument in memory of those who died in the Argonne (Architect Bollore, Sculptor Becker).

Monument to the Garibaldi units, raised in the village of La Chalade (Sculptor Cappabianca).

stalled their stronghold on the reverse slopes and in May, June and July they attempted further attacks ending in further defeats and appalling losses on both sides. The sector was highly disputed until the general offensive of the 20th August 1917, which completely cleared the left bank. Two divisions suffered particularly heavy casualties here: the 40th and the 69th, whose ex-servicemen have raised the monument known as *du Squelette* ("Skeleton"), the sculptor was Froment-Meurice.

Further west, Hill 304 and the fort at Marre constituted a line of defence with the access routes to Verdun in their cross-fire. The little Hill 304 was a constant menace to the Germans occupying the slopes of Mort-Homme; consequently from the start of April they moved to encircle the promontory, with the intention of capturing it at whatever cost. Until May and June, the artillery bombardment was so intense that the dust and smoke veiled the hill: 75 batteries concentrated their fire on a few hundred square metres. The Germans were unable to attain their goal. There was still brisk fighting in June and July 1917, the position was relieved from the 20th to 24th August 1917. 21 divisions won renown in this sector; 10,000 men were killed there. A committee of veterans who served at Hill 304, grouping together 35 Associations, has built a high pyramid bearing the units' numbers. (Architect Hamelin, sculptor Albert Lange).

THE ARGONNE

The Argonne, a hilly, wooded area between Champagne and the Meuse valley, was for a long time a frontier region between France and the Empire. Before the Americans' intervention in 1918, the Argonne was the scene of battles (1914-15) made particularly arduous by the fact that the ground there is largely clay. At that time the Germans wanted to

The American Memorial standing on Montfaucon hill. At the top of the tower — 58 m high — there is a statue of liberty.

A plan of the American attack. The chapel at Romagne-sous-Montfaucon cemetery. Thiaucourt cemetery. The remains of the church at Montfaucon. The Germans used the stones to build an observation post. Graves at Romagne-sous-Montfaucon cemetery. Montsec Monument.

reach the Chalons-Verdun railway and they attacked the Grurie woods and Haute Chevauchée ridge without respite. The cunning nature of the battle was augmented by the use of mines, which put the soldiers' nerves under severe strain. The Garibaldi batallion, made up of Italian volunteers, was brought to the front on the 26th December 1914. Sub-Lieutenant Bruno Garibaldi and one of his brothers, both grandsons of Guiseppe Garibaldi, fell in the first attacks. A monument sculptured by Cappabianca in memory of the Italians who came to fight and die side by side with the French has been raised in the village of La Chalade. The most intense offensives were in

July 1915, all along the road called *de la Haute Chevauchée,* an old Roman highway on the ridge — from Varennes to Les Islettes — in the forest of Argonne.

A monument in memory of the soldiers of the Argonne was erected in this vicinity. The architect was Bollore and the sculptor, Becker. There is an ossuary below the plinth.

THE AMERICANS

General Pershing's young American army particularly distinguished itself in the Meuse valley. Although it

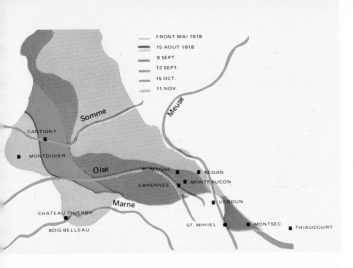

Romagne-sous-
Montfaucon cemetery.
The ornamental lake.

Aerial view.

The Memorial at Varennes-en-Argonne in honour of the soldiers of the State of Pennsylvania.

first took arms in the sector between Château Thierry and Bois Belleau in June 1918, it was at Saint-Mihiel and in the Argonne that the "Sammies" fully entered the battle, with the autonomous 1st American army whose strength was 550,000 men. On the 12th September 1918 the American divisions, supported by the French Colonial Corps, undertook the attack on the salient at Saint-Mihiel. Their success was absolute: in three days the Americans occupied the outcrop, took 16,000 prisoners and captured 440 guns. On the 26th September Pershing had 1,200,000 men, 2,500 guns and 325 tanks; he advanced his troops on a 24 km front between the Meuse and Argonne as part of the major offensive launched all along the front from Verdun to Ypres. The Americans entered Sedan on the 7th November. The American cemetery at Thiaucourt groups all those who died in the Battle of Saint-Mihiel: 4,152 graves. It is completed by the Montsec monument dominating the whole salient sector, with a marvellous bronze relief map aligned with the compass. The victims of the Meuse and Argonne battle repose in the cemetery at Romagne Sous Montfaucon: 14,246 graves. The American Memorial is at Montfaucon, 10 km away: a tower 58 m. high surmounted by a statue of liberty. The Americans have raised a memorial in honour of the soldiers from Pennsylvania State at Varennes, which they liberated on the 26th September 1918.

SAINT-MIHIEL

The town's name derives from an old abbey founded in 709 and dedicated to Saint Michael. Saint-Mihiel was a prosperous merchant and drapers' town in the Middle Ages; in the 14th century it became the seat of a sovereign court of justice called *"les Grands Jours."* The abbey also expanded at this time and the famous cardinal of Retz himself stayed there (although in exile) in the 17th century. The splendid buildings one may see today date from the 18th century, but the entrance porch to the abbey church displays a pure Romanesque style not dissimilar to Saint Vanne at Verdun.

Saint-Mihiel is best known as the home of Ligier Richier, the sculptor (Saint-Mihiel 1500-Geneva 1567). His *Virgin Mary in a Swoon* in the church of S Michael's abbey dates from 1531; but the most famous work is the *Holy Sepulchre* which he was not able to install himself (as a Protestant he was exiled) but which has been placed in Saint-Etienne church. This brilliant "image-maker" from Saint-Mihiel was just that: he knew how to feel and express the universality of his time and endow all his creations with intense life and restrained emotion. His oeuvre transcends the bounds of Renaissance in Lorraine, posing the eternal question of man's destiny.

Saint-Mihiel is particularly rich in Renaissance architecture and that of the classical centuries. The town has also inherited the important library collected by the Benedictines of S Michael's abbey. The bequest is still in its original place, it is kept in a very beautiful room on the first floor of one of the abbey's wings. The collections include miniatured manuscripts, incunabula and the first book printed in the Duchies, at Longeville devant Bar in 1502.

VARENNES-EN-ARGONNE

Whereas Saint-Mihiel — occupied by the Germans from 1914 to 1918 — suffered little permanent damage from its position as an outpost, the same is

The Sepulchre — Christ put in the Tomb — Ligier Richier's masterwork (Saint-Étienne Church, at Saint-Mihiel).

not true of Varennes. This old capital of the fief of the *Princes de Condé* (dependant upon Clermont) was severely shelled by the Germans, who occupied it in August-September 1914. When the French recaptured the town after the battle of the Marne, on the 15th September, it had been quite sacked. On the 22nd September, the Germans returned in force and took the town once again; they remained until the 26th September 1918.

It was, however, the arrest of King Louis XVI on the 21st June 1791 that made Varennes famous. We know that, after leaving *Les Tuileries* on the night of the 20th June 1791, the royal family made the mistake of separating from the energetic Fersen (he was suspected of being somewhat too intimate with Marie Antoinette) and furthermore travelled slowly with too

heavy a carriage. Finally, they lost precious time, which caused confusion in the military welcome party that had been set up from Pont de Sommevesle onwards; and the strange deployment of cavalry made the townships uneasy. At Sainte-Menehould the king was recognised by Drouet, the postmaster's son who had been a dragoon at Versailles and was to become a representative of the Republic's armies on campaign. Drouet was made prisoner by the Austrians, exchanged for Louis XVI's daughter Marie Thérèse when she was captive at Le Temple, and named sub-prefect of Sainte-Menehould by Napoleon before disappearing and dying mysteriously at Mâcon in 1827 (not without stirring up all the *gendarmeries* in the Meuse, for they thought they saw him everywhere...) At 11 p.m. the king was arrested in

The Musée d'Argonne *at Varennes (architect F. Delfour, D.P.L.G.), devoted to the arrest of Louis XVI and the end of the monarchy, the popular arts and traditions of Argonne and to the battles that took place there from 1914 to 1918, with in particular a striking reconstruction depicting mine warfare.*

Varennes by Sauce the grocer and mayor, aided by local patriots. Louis XVI was never to cross the Aire beyond which, by an irony of fate, a relay of horses and a squad of hussars were waiting for him at the *Auberge du Grand Monarque* so as to guard him on his way as far as Montmédy.

The arch below which the royal berlin came up against the improvised barricade erected by Drouet and the people of Varennes no longer exists; but the restored belfry which was contiguous is still there to recall the event. The little half-timbered house in the Argonne style where the royal family spent the night of the 21st June was destroyed by the shelling of 1914; a plaque records its site a few paces from the belfry.

The Museum of Argonne was opened in 1973, it stands on the edge of the forest in the high part of the little town. It was conceived and built to a modern design and offers the visitor vast rooms and well-lit galleries. Its purpose is double: to communicate the reality of contemporary Argonne and to highlight its historical past. The show-cases commemorate Louis XVI's journey, the war in the forest (there is a remarkable diorama illustrating the use of mines), the American intervention in 1918 and, finally, the art of china in Argonne, with an exceptional collection showing the variety and richness of its production, while at the same time allowing one to appreciate the sensitivity of the popular art of Argonne potters in the 18th and 19th centuries.

Varennes-en-Argonne: the Clock Tower reflected in the Aire. This is where Louis XVI was arrested: he never crossed the Aire.

Aerial view of Varennes-en-Argonne.

Aerial view of the Citadel at Montmédy.

MONTMEDY

This is a small, ancient fortress town built on a steep promontory overlooking the Chiers and Thonne valleys. The Count of Chiny erected a castle there around 1239. Montmédy was annexed to the duchy of Burgundy in 1444 and later passed into the possession of the Hapsburgs and of Spain. In 1657, when Louis XIV was 19 years old, he personally directed his first siege there, with the marshal of La Ferté. By passing through Louppy sur Loison, a charming little village a few kilometres from Montmédy, one may still admire the imposing Renaissance *château* where the king of France stayed during the siege. The treaty of the Pyrenees allocated the town to France in 1659 and Vauban revised its fortifications; they survive to this day, with two gates with drawbridges. In the high part of the town one may view an enormous dwelling called "the king's house": according to legend, Louis XVI was to stay there, surrounded by the marquis of Bouillé's royalist troops, if his flight had been a success... We know what became of him! The church, built in 1756, is scheduled as an historical monument. The visitor should not fail to go and see Avioth church, a magnificent Gothic building in pure French and Champagne style a few kilometres north of Montmédy: its admirable rose-window and doorway rise up in the austere Meuse landscape with an impressive, mystical effect.

Aerial view of the Avioth Basilica.

FRENCH, GERMAN AND AMERICAN NATIONAL CEMETERIES IN THE VERDUN AREA

43 French national cemeteries containing 80,726 identified bodies
29 German national cemeteries containing 54,845 identified bodies
2 American national cemeteries containing 18,398 identified bodies

French cemeteries

Ambly
Arrancy
Avocourt
Bar-Le-Duc
Belleray
Bras
Brieulles
Brocourt
Buzy
Chattancourt
Commercy
Dieue-Sur-Meuse
Dombasle-En-Argonne
Douaumont
Dugny
Eparges (Les) (Le Trottoir)
Esnes
Fromeréville
Haudainville
Islettes (Les)
Lachalade (La Forestière)
Lacroix-Sur-Meuse
Landrecourt (North and South)
Marbotte
Mont-Sous-Les-Cotes
Rembercourt-Aux-Pots
Revigny
Rupt-En-Woevre
Saint-Mihiel (Vaux-Racine)
Saint-Rémy
Senoncourt (Maujouy)
Sommedieue
Souhesmes (Fontaine-Routhon)
Trésauvaux
Troyon
Vadelaincourt
Vauquois
Verdun (Bévaux)
Verdun (Faubourg-Pavé)
Verdun (Glorieux)
Ville-Sur-Cousances

German cemeteries

Amel
Azannes 1 und 2
Brieulles
Bouligny
Cheppy
Consenvoye
Damvillers
Dannevoux
Dun-sur-Meuse
Epinonville
Hautecourt
Liny-devant-Dun
Marville
Lissey
Maizeray
Merles
Mangiennes
Montmédy
Nantillois
Peuvillers
Rembercourt
Romagne-sous-les-Côtes
Romagne-sous-Montfaucon
Saint-Maurice
Saint-Mihiel
Vaux-lès-Palameix
Viéville
Ville-devant-Chaumont

American cemeteries

Romagne-sous-Montfaucon
Thiaucourt

Contents

The printing of this book was completed
in the workshops of FISA - Industrias
Gráficas, Palaudarias, 26 - Barcelona
(Spain)

ACKNOWLEDGMENTS:

The Editors wish to thank all those people who have so kindly helped them, and would like to emphasise particularly
the assistance of Monsieur Gérard CANINI, University Agrégé, with the text. They also thank the "COMITE NA-
TIONAL DU SOUVENIR DE VERDUN," Monseigneur Pierre BOILLON, Bishop of Verdun, and Monseigneur
ROUYER, the Canon, for their help.

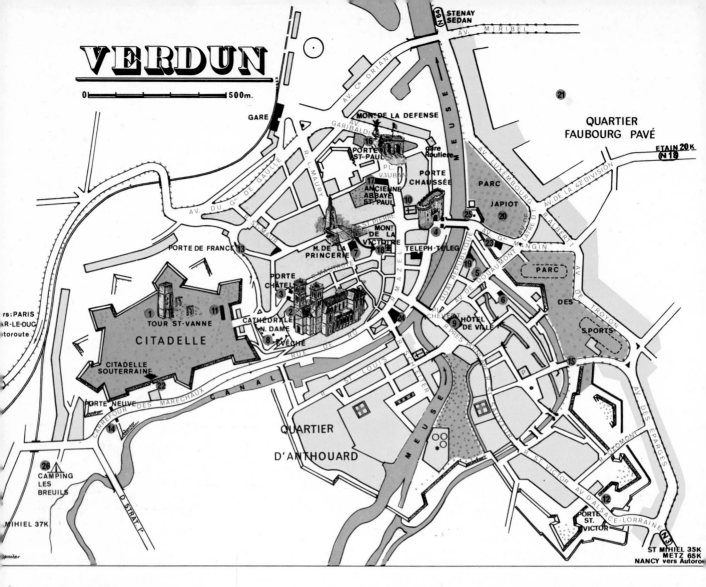

VERDUN

0 ____ 500m.

1 S Vanne Tower
2 Cathedral - Crypt - Cloister
3 Porte Châtel (Gate)
4 Porte Chaussée (Gate)
5 Tour des Plaids ("Litigation Tower")
6 Tour de l'Islot ("Islet Tower")
7 Musée de la Princerie (Museum)
8 Bishop's Palace
9 Hôtel de Ville (Town Hall)
10 Chapelle du Collège
11 High Citadel - Military Graves Bureau
12 Porte S Victor (Gate)
13 Porte de France (Gate)
14 Porte du Secours or Porte Neuve ("Gate of Help," or "New Gate") - Carrefour des Maréchaux ("Marshals' Crossroads")

15 Porte du Champ ("Field Gate")
16 Porte S Paul (Gate) - Defence Monument by Rodin
17 Former S Paul's Abbey - (Sub-Prefecture and Law Courts)
18 Victory Monument and Crypt
19 Officers' Club ("Cercle Militaire")
20 Parc Japiot (Park)
21 The Faubourg Pavé quarter
22 Entrance to the Underground Citadel
23 Syndicat d'Initiative
24 Theatre
25 Monument to the Fallen
26 Les Breuils Campsite

"La Défense" Monument, based on a model by Rodin. A French soldier and a German in 1916.